GW00480714

This Journal
Belongs To:

....

....

28269179R00068

Printed in Great Britain
by Amazon